07/18/2024

Blessings,

D. L. font

STORMS IN LIFE BRING
RICHER GROUND

SCHOOLHOUSE TO JAILHOUSE
-JAILHOUSE TO SCHOOLHOUSE

Based on a true life story

Written by:
DAVID JONATHAN

THOUGHTS TO PONDER

"Sow peace, kindness, knowledge and wisdom in the spring time. Continue to water each during the summer time. Reap plentiful in the autumn. Winter will be filled with friends and pleasant memories." DJ

"Wilderness memories must never be forgotten. Learn from them and grow. DJ

"But He knows the way I take; when he has tested me, I shall come forth as gold."
(KJV. Job 23:10)

DISCLAIMER

T his story is based on true life events and not meant to duplicate any other's life events. Names used throughout the book have been changed for protection. Any name(s) used have been made up by the author, for protection.

I have tried to recreate events, locations, and conversations from my memory. In order to maintain anonymity, in some instances, I have changed the names of individuals and places. I may have changed some identifying characteristics and details such as physical properties, occupations, and places of residence.

TABLE OF CONTENTS

ACKNOWLEDGMENTS

S pecial thanks to all who supported me through this devastating event.. The community shall remain nameless, to protect all involved. Thanks to God and you for sharing the electricity of life that brought me through.

Candy McCarley and her son, Jesse McCarley, for years of support and friendship.

Former Senator, John McKay, for his support through this ordeal.

Dr. Guetzloe, whom I may not agree with her ideology, but admire her stance about children when she stated, "What you expect from your students, you will get from your students."

Mr. and Mrs. Stoltz for all they did to assist me.

All the friends that helped me pack to move to Pennsylvania.

Mark Fromang, P.A., my attorney, through this event.

The churches in the surrounding areas.

Kenneth Clark, Senior Publishing Consultant, Xulon Press, for his persistence and prayerful approach in helping me towards publication.

Molly DeAndre, (She is with the Lord.), for her prayers and phone calls of concerns.

Christian Law Association for their referring me to a Christian attorney.

Joyce Meyer Association for their prayers.

Dr. and Mrs. Padronaggio for visiting me during the time I was incarcerated.

My beloved mother, Ethel Hubler, for all her prayers. She is with the Lord.

Tony and Maryann Laird for their friendship and editing support

Dr. David O. Olawale, who attends my church, City Church of Tallahassee, FL.

I know there are many, many more people that I did not mention. God knows who you are.

Fondly,
David Jonathan

INTRODUCTION

I could start out by saying that I was born into a small town in Pennsylvania in a three-bedroom, brown-shingled house, with a red tin roof, in 1949. Well, I was, so that's my start. However, stories, from that time of my life, are for another time and place. I'm skipping into the future to 1988.

I began teaching before 1988. However, 1988 is the year I started teaching at a public middle school in Florida. I taught 6th, 7th, and 8th grade, mostly made up of boys who were labeled EH/SED. When I signed on to teach the class, I had no idea what the EH/SED letters meant; so, I asked, and I was told that EH stood for Emotionally Handicapped and SED stood for Severely Emotionally Disabled. I thought, "I can teach students with handicaps such as: wheelchair bound, blind, etc." Surprise! The first day of school a student opened the door of the portable building, threw his backpack across the room, and slammed the door. His backpack hit the wall so hard that it made the whole portable shake. That made me sit up straight! Then he asked, "Who be you?" I introduced myself. He asked, "Where be the teacher from last year?" I informed him that the teacher was no longer working at this school. I was the new teacher. The student grunted in response. I had my work cut out for me.

The first two days of school were horrible. In fact, so horrible that I walked out of the classroom, left the school, and went to the beach with a friend of mine. I told her what happened and that I probably lost my job. This happened on a Thursday afternoon.

I sheepishly returned back to the school the following morning Monday morning. As I came into the front office area, the Principal pulled me by my shirt back to her office and said "David, all that I am asking you to do is to keep those students out of the halls. Keep them in your classroom and out of my office. Can you do that?" I said that I could. She told me to get back to work.

Before I had a chance to leave her office, she asked, "How long have you been working with kids?"

I answered, "About 10 years."

She asked, "Ever had any trouble, in your life, because of kids?"

I was startled by the question, and I answered, "No. Why?"

"David," she responded, "When you work with kids, your time will come."

I looked at her, puzzled by her comment, and thought, "Nah, not me."

I never knew what the Principal meant until "The Event," which I am about to tell you happened in my life. How did she predict "The Event?"

May 24th, 2000
9:58 AM

Chapter I

EVENTS AS REMEMBERED

On Wednesday, April 26th, about 4 PM, I was called to the Principal"s office, at the middle school. Upon arriving at the office, I was introduced to two private investigators from the Childrens' Division of the Sheriff's Office. Their names were Susan and Earl. They instructed me to come with them.

I followed them outside and down the walkway to the Crimes against Childrens' Offices. We talked about the weather as we walked. It was a beautiful spring day in Florida. I have been accustomed to being called into the Childrens' Division of the Sheriff's Department, on numerous occasions, to discuss certain incidents or behaviors of a particular youth that I was mentoring, or the youth was a participant in my not-for-profit Christian youth-based organization. However, on this partic-ular day, one detective walked in front of me, and the other one walked behind me. I felt this was different, and something was wrong.

They did not take me into the main office of the Childrens' Division. Instead, they opened another door a few doors down from the main door. I followed them through a maze of aisles back to a small room. They opened the door and took me to a seat. The room was stark. I noticed a huge dark bubble hanging at the back, of the room, in the upper corner. I figured that that bubble contained a camera. Earl sat in the middle of the room. Susan told me to have a seat at the table that was in front of the room. I still had no idea why I was there. In fact, I believe I remember asking why was I there? Susan told me that she would let me know in a few minutes.

As promised, within a few minutes, Susan opened a folder and sat down at the table with me. She leaned forward and got right in my face. She began to ask questions about how I got my youth to participate in my program. She stared at me directly into my eyes. I stared back directly into her eyes. She began to say something about sleepovers. She put her face approximately four inches away from my face. I began to feel like I was in another world. I still had no idea why I was in this room being interrogated and, now, in front of these two detectives. I will try, though I find it hard to express myself, at this time, to continue, with the event. .

Susan also began to make innuendos about my behavior with children. I remembered looking directly at her. I kept my eyes fixed directly into her eyes. I realized, at that moment, a kid had made a complaint about me. My mind began to whirl with the names of all the kids that I had to bring before the courts because of their violations of agreed behaviors. Most of the youth that I worked with had been in trouble with the law. Some were assigned to me from the County's "Teen Court" or they were referred to me. The referrals would come from parents or from other kids that I already worked with, or from people hearing about my organization on the two radio programs; or, the two TV programs. Kids also come from the juvenile court system to do service hours with my organization. I really did not know what Susan was trying to insinuate. Everything she was saying was false, but she wanted me to believe it was true. All were false accusations! Susan wanted so badly for me to confess to things that I did not do. At one point, she called me a "liar" to my face. I was not lying! The little girl was the liar! I remembered thinking, "I'm cornered!" I never dreamed a kid would turn on me like this. I prayed inwardly. "Oh God, please help me. You know this is not true. I need your help now, in Jesus'name, amen." A peace came over me. I knew my Heavenly Father, God Himself, was with me. He knew my heart. I was not lying. I was not guilty of any of these accusations.

> "I cried unto God with my voice, even unto
> God with my voice, and He gave ear unto me."
> (Psalms 77:1).

Then, she asked me if I knew of a girl named MaLinda. I told her that I had. Susan began to accuse me of having some type of sexual relations, with her, beginning when she was 10 years old! I believe Susan used the words lewd and lascivious acts. Next, Susan accused me of having "sleepovers with girls" at my house. That was false. Then she mentioned something about charging me with molestation. Susan even talked about having sex with permission between the girl and

17

myself. Susan's spit sprayed my face as she screamed into it. (I remembered thinking that at least her breath did not smell; however, the words that were coming out of her mouth stank). I stared Susan directly into her eyes and repeatedly said, "No!"

"Oh my God," I remember thinking that MaLinda was the last person I ever dreamed would accuse me of doing something so foul. I thought she was a Christian girl. How could she tell such bold face lies? What I did for about one hour in the home, at the request and presence of her grandmother, was try to help her through the troubled suicidal period of her life. And this is the thanks I get?! When Susan mentioned the girl's name, I could not believe it. I wanted to fall off the chair in disbelief! I could not believe that MaLinda would accuse me of such degrading and violating acts against her. I have never degraded or violated MaLinda, but she has now violated and degraded me by defaming and smearing the very nature of my character! I do forgive her. May God in His mercy forgive her, also.

As I stared directly into Susan's eyes, I could see and feel her hatred toward me. What Susan was saying was totally false. I "pray" with kids. I do not "prey" on them. I remember thinking, "What would Jesus do in a situation like this?" Jesus would keep his mouth shut. So, I stopped trying to defend myself except for continually repeating the word "No!" to every allegation.

At one point during the interrogation, I was trying to explain that all I wanted to do was "to reach out to touch the family with help." Susan started to jump all over me, because I had used the word "touch." Everything I tried to say to defend myself was being twisted around and used against me. That was the very reasoning the attorneys used when they gave me the advice not to take a polygraph test. They told me that no matter how innocently I tried to explain myself, the detectives would twist the statements around and use them against me. They advised me that if the detectives wanted a polygraph test, they (the attorneys) would give me one themselves. The attorneys also informed me that the fact the detectives allowed me to leave, after the interrogation, meant that they really had no solid proof or probable cause of the allegations, or I would have been handcuffed, arrested, and hauled off to jail. The allegations, if true and provable, were a capital offense. I could be facing up to 125 years in federal prison!

I felt like I had died!

Susan outright accused me of having sexual relations with Malinda. When I said, "No, I did not," Susan called me a liar. I felt drained, embarrassed, belittled, and like I was all of a sudden living in another world. I felt like this was not really happening, but it was, and it did happen!

At one point, the two detectives left the room. I was left to sit there by myself. I had some referrals that I had written in my classroom on two girls that has misbehaved. The referrals were not completely finished. So I continued filling out the information needed on the behavioral referrals. I knew I was being attacked, but I did not know why. Still, a part of me thought that the detectives would come back into the room, apologize to me, and tell me that I was the wrong man and thank me for my cooperation. I was quite perplexed, but I was not nervous. I knew I was innocent. I knew I had never done this.

Earl came into the room alone. He proceeded to tell me that he knew I was a Christian man (praise the Lord!). He told me that he would be very disappointed in me if, in fact, he found out that these allegations were true. He sat down in the chair where Susan had been sitting, at the table, but he was much softer spoken. He did not lean forward in the chair, and he did not get in my face. In fact, he spoke kindly, yet firmly. I remember telling him that because I am a Christian man, I am very much aware of the verse found in Matthew (18:6) that stated if I were to cause one of these little ones to stumble, it would be like hanging a millstone around my neck and drowning in the sea. I told him that I worked very hard in this community to keep my name clean. It had taken me years, but I had finally earned the community's trust and respect, especially from the family of this little girl. I encouraged parents to search me out. It is an awesome responsibility for a parent to entrust their child, especially these days, to anyone. In fact, just a couple of weeks ago, I used the grandmother as a reference for a family that wanted me to work with their two children. Why would I do this if I were doing something to the girl, that would prove me untrustworthy? I thought the grandmother trusted me. She always told me that she did. I valued her trust in me. In fact, I was the oldest granddaughter's tutor in algebra. The grandmother trusted me with a lot of damaging "gossip" of people involved with her, in her political career. What is the reason I would break her trust?

I told Earl, of the time approximately two years earlier, the grandmother had called me to come over to the house to speak to her granddaughter, MaLinda. She explained to me that MaLinda's elementary school had informed her that MaLinda was demonstrating angry behavioral and suicidal tendencies.

The grandmother also said that she did not know who MaLinda was talking to or why the school would say such a thing about her granddaughter. Since I am a Behavioral Specialist, the grandmother thought that I could talk to the girl. I was asked to give my professional opinion and my thoughts on the possibilities of MaLinda committing or not committing suicide. The grandmother told me that she did not trust the elementary school's concerns, nor did she trust their judgements of the testing procedures and testing instruments. I went to the house. The grandmother was present and gave me permission to talk to MaLinda in the dining room. I discussed with MaLinda concerns of mood swings, her behavior with her talking about suicide. I was told, by the grandmother, that MaLinda's father had molested the two older sisters.

I talked with MaLinda, for approximately thirty monutes. MaLinda told me that she was not going to commit suicide. I prayed with her. She told me about the scars that she has on her chest, because she had tried several times in the past to commit suicide. (I mentioned this, also, to Dectective Susan who outright accused me of seeing those scars. I have never seen nor have the desire to see MaLinda's scars on her chest). The dining room where we talked was an open area, and the grandmother was in the kitchen preparing supper as we talked. At the end of the discussion, MaLinda and I prayed again.; then, MaLinda went back to her room.

I also informed Dectective Susan that MaLinda told her story, including the scarring of the breast area on one of my "Bible Brunch" radio programs. Everyone was shocked that MaLinda would reveal publicly on the radio such private matters she and

I discussed at her home, but this was MaLinda's way of crying out for help. She was hurt and confused back then. None of us was sensitive enough to her cries. She wanted one of us to rescue her from the pain. Something was bothering her then, but we failed to listen.

Finally, Earl and Susan came back into the room together. They had a blood search warrant. I could read the blood search warrant and it said that it was for genital warts. At the time, I remembered studying about genital warts in a class of health science at college. I could not remember exactly what they looked like or how they affected the genital area. I told the detectives that whatever the warts were, I didn't have any-thing in my genital area that resembled warts. I told them that they had the wrong man. But I cooperated. I had to. I had no choice. I put out my right arm, and they withdrew blood into two lavender topped tubes. Also, The blood search warrant stated that they were to search me physically, in other words, look at my body to see if I had genital warts. They did not do that.

About this time, I felt shell-shocked. I felt like I had died. I felt like I was knocked out. Everything felt so unreal. I knew the truth that I was not guilty of any of these assusations, but I was scared because I felt so helpless and so condemned. God in his mercy was looking out for me right then. I believe I kept my cool, because I knew my God knew the truth. This struck me from left field. Inwardly I began to pray. I was so sure that the girl's grandmother did not know anything about her grand-daughter's false accusations against me. Earl told me not to go near the girl or contact the girl in any way. I was free to go.

During the interrogation, I was scared I would be going to jail for something I did not do. I knew that the charges were serious, but at the time, I did not realize just how serious and what the consequences were. I later found out that I could receive up to 125 years in federal prison.

I left the room confused, bewildered, and disoriented. The first thing I did was to go back to the school's administration office to see if the Principal was still at the school. She had already left for the day. Being so disoriented, I remember going around in circles, not knowing exactly who to talk to or where to go. I had to talk to the grandmother. I just knew that she would understand. She knew her granddaughter had problems. I have known the grandmother for a number of years and worked with her on cases similar to this at The Glens, a local private organization that works with families and troubled adolescents. The Glens is where I first met the grandmother. That was about ten years ago. She worked as a caseworker. The grandmother later served as Acting President of my not-for-profit youth organization, Education Helps, Inc.

On April 26, 2000, I died. The old energetic, creative, willing to help, always happy, and always ready to begin to dig in and fight man was dead. I was scared that day. I did not realize that the fact that they let me go meant that they really had no real evidence with which to hold me. It was her word against my word. I had never before experienced anything like the feelings that I felt that day.

*

Chapter II

WHAT A DAY MAY BRING FORTH

Then day began just like any other day of my life, but it had a tragic ending. That's what I thought at that time. Little did I realize that what I thought was a tragedy, God would mold into "all things working together for good." Keep reading and allow me to share the great things that God has done. One never knows what a day may bring forth.

Where was I? Oh yes. The last time MaLinda was on the radio program, "Bible Brunch," was August 1999. Crystal, her grandmother, picked her up after the program. MaLinda has never been to my home. I was never alone with her in any of my cars, at anytime. The detectives said that MaLinda told them that I had led her to believe I was much younger than I really was. MaLinda, as do all the kids, know that I am "one day younger than water." When I was acting as youth pastor at a Baptist Church, where MaLinda frequently attended, the kids celebrated my 49th birthday. I do not know how old MaLinda told the detectives that she thought I was. She was untruthful even about that part; she knew my age. I have never hidden my age from any of the kids. My silver hair would give my age away.

MaLinda revealed on a "Teen Talk" program about how the boys at her elementary school put small razors in their mouths, which they used to threaten girls to have sex with them, in the bathrooms. Everyone thought that was an unbelievable story, but none of us proceeded to check the story out. As I look back, I believe MaLinda was again crying out for help. Also, MaLinda's older sisters, who had been molested by their father, told how they were afraid to go to the bathrooms at their high school because of threats from other girls to have lesbian sex with them. Crystal was well aware of all of this. We did discuss this matter and the grandmother thought it was a shame on the schools. This too was brought up on a "Teen Talk" program. There are witnesses who remember these stories. The Chief of Police was on the "Teen Talk" program when these stories were discussed.

Another thing the girl told the detectives was that she did not know about my name change from Hubler to Jonathan. This, too, was another lie that MaLinda told. On May 2nd, I gave the detectives two tapes of radio programs where MaLinda and Crystal were present. On the one tape of a "Teen Talk" program, I played a tape from a kid who had threatened to blow up my classroom one morning when I turned on the light switch. On the tape, the student called me "Mr. Hubler." After playing the tape, I explained on the radio program the reason why that particular student called me "Mr. Hubler." I explained my name change in the radio studio. Both the grandmother and the girl were present.

I had a copy of a "Bible Brunch" program where MaLinda states that most of her friends are suicidal and come to her for help. This was about two years ago, 1998. Looking back, I believe that, at the time, MaLinda and her sisters were crying out for help, but we did not pay enough attention to that possibility. The grandmother would not heed my advice.

How lonely I feel right now. I know God is with me, I am never alone. I am used to having the phones ringing and always doing something for someone. Since this situation, my ministry has basically shut down. There are no more radio programs. No more youth coming to Bible studies. No more jail ministry, and no more Saturday morning nursing home ministry visits, with the kids. It is even hard for me to continue to write this book, because I feel like I am reliving the whole thing over again. This is so painful. However, I have a deep inner strength that my God will never leave me nor forsake me. The same goes for you. When you trust in God as your Heavenly Father, through Jesus Christ, nothing is impossible.

After I had spoken to MaLinda in her home, she drew a picture for me. The grandmother was present when MaLinda gave me the picture. Crystal said that MaLinda was up during the middle of the night drawing the picture. Up to this time, I did not know that MaLinda could draw. MaLinda and Crystal told me that MaLinda had never previously drawn this good. MaLinda told me that she had a vision, and in the vision she saw Jesus with his hand over my head, as I knelt before Him. Jesus was saying, "David, I'll always be with you." I did not realize MaLinda called me David." I have a rule: a kid may call me Mr. Jonathan or "Mr. J" until he/she is 18 years old.

When the child graduates high school, receives a diploma, and remains drug free, then, and only then, may he/she call me by my first name "David."

MaLinda and Crystal were so proud of the drawing that I was led to believe that MaLinda had not drawn before that time. I have found out since that MaLinda had drawn pictures before. I gave the detectives the original drawing, and two original tapes of where MaLinda knew of my name change and where she says that most of her "friends are suicidal and come to her for help." I gave the detectives these items on May 2, 2000, a Tuesday.

After the interrogation on April 26, I was determined to prove that I was innocent. The detectives had a search warrant for my blood to see if I had genital warts. The detectives also kept floundering between genital warts and genital herpes. However, the search warrant said genital warts. Not to worry, I have neither disease. I willingly gave the blood. I wanted to take the polygraph test to prove my innocence. A polygraph test was originally scheduled for May 5th at 8 a.m. Later, Earl, the Dective, called me and said, "Good news, the polygraph has been rescheduled to Tuesday, May 2nd, at 8 A.M."

Do you remember reading about how distraught and disoriented I felt after the interrogation on April 26th? When I drove home, I felt like I was in another world. I was so distraught and troubled concerning the false accusations that were made against me. I did not realize I could be so mistreated and so degraded as an innocent man. I came home from the interrogation and took such a long, hot shower. I felt so dirty, violated, and perverted. I guess I took such a long shower, because I was so stunned and shocked that this little girl would accuse me of something so dirty. In true Christian love, I reached out to her and her family. I listened to her, prayed with her, and pointed her to the Savior. I just knew that her grandmother, a Godly woman, would not believe her granddaughter's report, but instead would work together with me so that we could help her granddaughter and get to the bottom of MaLinda's problems. Who did what to her? When did this occur? And why was she blaming it on me? After all, it was the grandmother who told me about the father's incest on the other two granddaughters. The grandmother told me that she was not really sure, but she did not believe the father molested MaLinda.

In retrospect, I remember after the discussion in the home with the girl concerning her reported suicidal thoughts, deep down, I knew something seriously bothered her. I suggested the grandmother seek psychiatric help, for MaLinda. The grandmother did not want her granddaughter, whom she raised, be placed in an institution like The Glens. Also, at the time, I remember thinking that there was a great possibility that the father had molested MaLinda. or, the girl may be sexually active and afraid to tell her grandmother. It was possible that someone else had molested the girl. I did share that with the grandmother. The grandmother refused to listen to any of my suggested possibilites. I have been told that statistics prove that if incest takes place in a family, the family perpetrator does not usually stop with just one of the children. Something terrible had occurred to this little girl, but it was not done by me.

The evening of April 26th, after Bible study, I called the grandmother's home, spoke directly to the grandmother and not to MaLinda.. This is true from April 26th up to the present. Calling the home was a big mistake! The detectives told me during the interrogation not to discuss this investigation with any member of the family. I, honestly, cannot remember this directive from the detectives. I do remember them telling me not to go near the girl or talk to the girl. Most importantly, God knows my heart. If the detectives did tell me not to talk to any member of the family, after the interrogation, the tape of the interrogation would be the only proof. I guess it really does not matter, at this point. The fact is, I did call twice and talked only to the grandmother. Here is good advice to you reading this book. If you ever go through an interrogation of any kind, for any reason, do not discuss anything with anyone until it is made public record and/or the investigation is over.

It is really hard for me to relive this situation through the writing of this book, but I will continue on with God's strength. I believe this story has to be told. It must be told not only to help someone who may be in a terrible situation, but to the honor and glory of Jesus Christ. I also promised Him that I would publish what great thing God has done. I will take a deep breath and continue.

**

Chapter III

THE GRANDMOTHER

I have visited and prayed with the grandmother during a hospital stay of hers. I thought that I had developed a good Christian rapport. I have even attended her church, a Missionary Baptist Church, to worship with her and her granddaughters on several occasions.

On April 26, 2000, right after the interrogation, I phoned the Grandmother, and the grandmother answered the phone, I remember asking her if she knew what was up with MaLinda. She told me that all she knew was MaLinda was talking to a teacher at school and that two people stopped by the house to talk with her. Other than that, she did not know anything. I informed her that MaLinda told detectives I had sexually abused her. Crystal seemed dumbfounded just about as much as I was. I asked Crystal to talk to MaLinda, to pray with her, and for her to tell the truth so the case could be dropped against me. I did not beg the grandmother to do this. The grandmother made the remark that if she for one moment thought that I was guilty of any sexual misconduct, with her granddaughter, she would not be talking to me now. She said that she would talk with MaLinda and find out what information she could. I made no threats to her, MaLinda, or any member of the family. The granddaughter did not answer the phone nor did I ask to speak with her. I instinctively wanted to talk to the grandmother. I just knew that, between the two of us, we could get to the bottom of the situation. I wanted her to find out why MaLinda would tell such lies against me. At this point, I still had no idea of the complete allegations that MaLinda had brought against me. The grandmother made the remark that she could not even remember a time when I was ever alone with her granddaughter. Since that time, I have searched my brain, and I still cannot come up with any time that I was ever alone with the girl. I have inquired of the other kids that formerly participated in the Bible studies and radio programs. They agreed that there was always someone, in the car, with me, whenever I stopped by to pick up the girl. The few instances that I dropped her back at her house, the kids also stated there was always one them in the car with me. The grandmother and I discussed that there always were other kids, with me, at all times when I would come by the house to pick up or return her granddaughter. I kept a close watch on any of her granddaughters to protect them from the boys. The grandmother agreed with this information.. I asked if I could call next evening to find out if she had talked to the MaLinda. The grandmother gave me permission to do so. We both said our goodbyes.

***

Chapter IV

THE ALLEGATIONS

April 27, 2000

This was a Thursday. Upon arriving at school, I informed the Principal of the allegations made against me last evening. A few minutes later, the Principal called me back to her office. She told me that I was suspended without pay until further notice pending the investigation. After getting a few personal items and making lesson plans for the substitute teacher, I left the school.

Later in the afternoon, I called the grandmother back to see what she had found out,, from MaLinda. The grandmother answered the telephone. Again, I never asked to speak to the girl, nor did I threaten in any way. The grandmother told me that her granddaughter had mentioned my name, and the granddaughter told the detective that I did these things. I just knew by the questioning and insinuating remarks, at the interrogation, I was labeled a "child molester." This was a serious matter. I was being labeled and treated as if I was guilty. I am innocent, but now I have to prove that I am innocent! What has happened to our judicial system?

I believed in the grandmother and I thought that she truly believed in me. I did ask the grandmother to pray with the girl, so that MaLinda would stop lying and tell the truth. If the truth were told, the case against me would be dropped. I informed the grandmother that I had been suspended from my job without pay, and I stood to lose everything that I had so diligently worked for. The grandmother sighed. She then stated that if all of this was false, then there was going to be "an awful lot of forgiveness to be had." The grandmother then stated that she did not believe that I did this. She also remarked again that if she thought I had done this, she would be talking to me. Her remark had reassured me of the grandmother's confidence and trust in me. I, at that point , believed that the grandmother knew that I was not guilty. The grandmother stated that she would talk again with her granddaughter. During this phone call, I remember discussing with the grandmother the case that we worked on together at The Glens. I would like to share that "little storm" with you, at this time.

I was a respite worker at The Glens. I was working with a fifth grade boy. He needed help with schoolwork, and, so, I thought we could go to a nearby park, sit at a picnic bench, and we could work on his math homework. It was a beautiful day in Florida. The weather was perfect. There were other people at the park, but the area we picked was quiet, although it was out in the open. While I was working with this kid, he made the comment that his teacher told him that he would fail his Human Growth and Development class, if he did not see an adult male's private parts. I was shocked by his remarks. I asked him who his teacher was. He told me. I told him that I did not think that his teacher would make such an assignment. He insisted that she did.

I tried to return our focus to his math homework, but the boy was obsessed with his "so-called" assignment for Human Growth and Development class. He got up from the bench. He began to run around the bench repeating that he was going to fail unless he fulfilled this assignment. He insisted that I could be that adult male, and I would help him pass his class. I said to myself, "Oh dear God, how in the world did I ever get myself into this predicament." The boy kept running around in circles touching me on the shoulders every time as he passed by me. I thought it about time we left the park and head back to his house. The biggest question was, how to get this boy into my truck and home, without him causing a scene? The boy kept insisting that he could take me somewhere to fulfil this assignment. I kept telling him "No." I instructed him to get into my truck. To my pleasant surprise, he listened to me!

Traveling to his home seemed to take forever. The boy kept telling me all the places we could go where we could complete the assignment. I kept a straight trek toward his home. At one intersection, he proceeded to tell me that we could go into the bathroom at a gas station, on the corner. I turned to him and asked, "You've done this before haven't you?" The boy did not answer me. We came to a red traffic light. An eighteen-wheeler pulled up alongside of us. I could see that the truck driver had a clear vision into my truck. At this point, the boy told me that he could take his pants down right here, and I could take mine down also. I firmly commanded the boy, "Don't you even dare!"

I remember thinking that I could see the headlines of the newspaper: TEACHER CAUGHT IN TRUCK WITH BOY'S PANTS DOWN! I began to panic, but we were only about a mile away from the boy's house. I remember praying, "Oh Lord, please let his parents be at home."

We pulled into the boy's driveway and his sister came running out of the house. She asked, "Why were we home so early?" I asked her if her parents were home. She told me, "No." She told me that they should be home shortly. The only went to the store for a few items; they should be right back. The sister asked me if something was wrong. I told her that I needed to speak to the parents.

The boy was getting a little anxious. He wanted to leave my truck and run. I reached over and held him in the truck by grasping onto the seat belt. Thank God that his parents pulled up behind my truck within few minutes.

.I told them I had to speak to them immediately, and they invited me into the house. I told them I wanted the boy to be with us also. I proceeded to tell them about all that happened at the park. The mother seemed very hurt. The stepfather left the room and, I believe, he went upstairs. The boy did not deny anything. The mother looked very distraught. She began to cry. She told me this was not the first time that her son had tried this with an adult male. She stated that there was another counselor who she believed had fallen into her son's trap and did have some kind of sexual conduct with her son. However, he left town and moved to Canada. The mother told me that she suspected her husband might be doing something sexually with her son. (I, too, suspected that about her husband.

He acted strangely in my opinion). She cried bitterly. I told her that I would get her son help. I left the home and returned to The Glens to report the incident.

The reason that I told this story at this point, is because the grandmother of the little girl, who accused me, was my supervisor at The Glens. I sat with the Supervisor and told her what occurred during my respite time with the little boy. I wrote a six-page report about the incident. The Supervisor was impressed by how I handled the situation. That was where and when I thought my Supervisor and I had become friends. She stated that she wanted me to meet her granddaughters, because they had problems. I told her I would be happy to meet them, in her presence, and help them with their problems, if I could.

A Staff meeting was called, at the boy's school, to discuss how best we could help this child. I was invited to the Staffing. I walked into the room. The boy was not sitting in his chair. I asked where he was. The man conducting the meeting told me that he was under the table. He was refusing to sit in his chair. I told them that no kid is going to run any staffing that I attend. Upon stating that remark, I bent down, looked under the table and told the boy to get to his seat or I was going to tell the people at this meeting everything that had happened during our respite time. The boy quickly jumped up into his seat. The man turned to me and asked how did I achieve that? I informed him that I was the adult, the boy was the child. I, as the adult, was in control. (I have always operated like that and I still do. I show respect to a child, and he/she will do likewise to me). A few years later I met the boy in the local Shopping Mall. He was then 15 or 16. He came over to me, shook my hand and apologized for his actions years ago. I could not believe that he remembered the event. He told me that he had become a Christian, and he thanked me for helping him.

I hope this explains the reason why I had to telephone the grandmother and ask for her help immediately. After all, it was the grandmother who came to me to ask me to help her with her granddaughter's suicidal problems and the other granddaughter's incest problems. The grandmother has told me time and time again that she admired the way the kids showed respect to me and how I showed respect back to them. To show that line of respect, the kids will call me "Mr. J." They will not call me by my first name. I know from my heart, at least I still want to believe that the grandmother from the onset of her granddaughter's accusations against me, knew they were false and a result of her granddaughter's previous problems. This little girl was also upset because her real mother lived two doors down the street from her, but her mother never came to see her. I do believe that the grandmother knew her granddaughter was lying about me, but she was willing to sacrifice my name and job to protect the "family secret" of incest problems. Her family's name and political career were on the line. Rather than to seek help for her granddaughter and show concern for the granddaughter, she would protect the family's name. How sad. It hurts me deep inside because of all the pain and suffering that I will endure for the rest of my life. Only through God's strength do I continue to live.

The one thing that really baffles me is the fact that on the word of a 12-year-old girl, without any solid proof or concrete evidence, my word had no bearing. To God be the glory! He knows the truth. I am free. I continually pray that the little girl, after all, will come to know God as I do as Abba Father. After all, the girl does not have a real earthly daddy. I believe all kids need a loving, godly father, who has earned the right to be called, "my daddy."

As I went through this major storm in my life, at times it is hard to keep focused. Mentally, I am strained. Physically, I tend to tire easily. I go through moments of paranoia and even times where I become an introvert. You, also, may be experiencing these emotional lows. Those are the times you must call out for spiritual help from someone you can trust. They will minister to you at your lowest ebb of life. Even now, there are times when I break down and weep. This is easier said than done, but I've got to stop fixing my eyes on the circumstance that is around me and, instead, focus on the One who surrounds me! Stop reading this book, if you must, and go into silent prayer. It will help you. I have ceased from my writing to do just that. I don't mind you continuing to read, if this book strengthens you. My prayer is that it does; then, read on. Here are two verses that may help to strengthen you: "Thou will keep him/her in perfect peace whose mind is stayed on thee, because he/she trusts in thee. Trust ye in the Lord forever, for in the Lord God is everlasting strength." (Isaiah 26:3-4). KJV

****

Chapter V

PITY PARTY TIME

September 23rd, 2000

9:05 A.M.

I am having a difficult time writing this book. However, writing this book is a good way to release my feelings and share them with you. You, too, will go through zenith moments in the abyss. Let me explain myself.

Last night, I felt the Detectives were going to come to get me again. I have trouble driving around in my damaged car. Yes, I had an accident with my car during this situation, and I was not covered by insurance. I'll explain that later. Even my dreams are affected by this situation. Sometimes I have good dreams and other times they are nightmares. It got to the point yesterday that I could not continue writing this book. Television was boring. Reading was boring. My life is hapless and boring. I sat on my reclining chair, and I went into prayer. I felt even God was displeased and bored with me. I know deep down this is not true, but I am going through my "pity party time."

Several years ago, I went through an attorney to change my name. I paid the fee required and did everything legally through an attorney's office. I have always wanted the name of David Jonathan. I guess I thought when I gave my life to Christ, I would use my new name and drop my old name. I always felt there was a "curse" on my birth last name of "Hubler." I don't know why I felt that way. As a teenager, I was not close to my father. However, as I grew older, especially when I truly and totally gave my heart to Jesus Christ, I was drawn closer to my earthly Dad, and I developed a special love for him. I thought if I changed my last name, I could wipe my "teenager" memories of my father away. I was wrong. When Christ changed my life, He changed me from within. Birth names don't have any "curse" attached to them, in my opinion. It does not matter, to Jesus Christ, what my name was or is. Christ cared about my change from within. A change of heart causes a change from within; therefore, my outward actions have changed. My definition of love has changed. That's what Christ did for me. I asked for His mercy on my life and gave my heart to Him: I gave my "heart" to Him. Then I became a "liver" for Jesus! For me to live is Christ! During this situation I have become closer to my family. I have asked God's forgiveness, but I do believe it does not matter to Him what my last name is here on earth. I have a new name "written down in Glory!"

I had written a reading program under the name of David Jonathan. I used the name so the students would not know that their teacher wrote the program. I wanted the reading program to be a reliable program. It was and the school wote a check out to David Jonathan. I could not cash the check until I had

had the name David Jonathan legalized. I cashed the check and the rest is history. After this incident, I felt it would be to my advantage to keep my name as David Jonathan. I like my name! My name change occurred in 1991.

After my dad died in 1992, I believe wanting to carry through with my name change was a form of rebellion toward my father. I thought it would give me a sense of freedom from his tyrannical rule. My dad was a true Christian man. His rule was by the Bible. He loved us, so he warned us of the consequences of sin. I was the stupid one for not listening to my dad. My dad was a man of wisdom. My dad's wisdom was from God. God is wise. Thank God. The older I get the more I find myself becoming the imitation of my dad. I long to be as close to God as my dad was.

Now, I will go back to the event and share my jail time.

*****

Chapter VI

05/27/00 – 11:13 P.M.

Truly, the only one who really cares and understands is Jesus. Father God, I can no longer bear this burden of false accusations. Please hear my humble cries.

Jail Time

The detectives put me in the back seat of their plain colored green car. The handcuffs tightened up so much so that all I could do was to curl up on that back seat in a fetal position. The pain was profusely excruciating. A grown man humiliated and being hauled off to jail like a pig.

I still had no idea of the charges against me at this point.

After a few miles, from my house, the car came to a stop. The detectives got out of the car, opened the back door, pulled me out, made me walk with my head down and hunched over to the back seat, of a marked deputy's car. I was caged up inside the car. I noticed we were in front of the County Court House. The car was not running. All the doors and windows were shut. I was hot! The detectives and the deputy talked over the top of the car, for what seemed to me, a long time. Finally, Detective Susan opened up the front passenger side door, poked her head inside the car and stated, "You're going to jail for tampering with a witness." (She had papers in her hand). "Your bond is set at $10,000, for now! She backed her torso out of the car and slammed the door closed.

I yelled, "Why? What crime has been committed? Where's the witness?" My yelling was to no avail. Quietly, I returned to the fetal position, on the back seat of the patrol car.

When the deputy who was driving me to the jail returned, he turned around and said, "Well, you're going to the big house [jailhouse]!

******

Chapter VII

MAY'S DAYS

O 5/01/00–This is the day I saw Attorney Moss in Clearwater, FL. She seemed confused about what was happening, never saw a blood search warrant, and advised me not to take the polygraph with the sheriff's department on 05/02/2000. If anything I did, she said, was to cancel the polygraph.

Later that evening I took Attorney Moss' legal advice and left a message for the detectives that I would not show up for the polygraph test on, 05/02/00, at 8:00 a.m.

05/02/00 – 8:10 a.m. -I got a call from the polygraph man. He, apparently, had not received the message I left the last evening, of 05/01/00, that I was not to take the polygraph due to legal advice. We talked for a while. I told him that I would stay in touch with the detectives since I did not do anything to the girl (MaLinda).

In the afternoon of 05/02/2000, MaLinda called me , at my home. During MaLinda's phone calls, I could hear, in the background, the sound of a recording device; so; I knew that the

Detectives were taping our conversation. The Detectives had MaLinda call me.

05/03/00 – I received a phone call from MaLinda. During the course of MaLinda's call to me, she stated that I had called her Saturday (04/29/00) and that I called her a "slut." Check the phone records – I did not call MaLinda a "slut." During the two calls that I admitted to Crystal, I spoke directly to Crystal, the grandmother. I did not call the house Saturday 04/29/00 – more importantly, I never spoke to MaLinda during this time of investigation from 04/26/00 until now. On 04/29/00, I went to the nursing home, in the morning, as I usually did, to visit with the patients. From there, I drove up to the Polk City Youth Development Center (YDC) for a pre-scheduled visit with the Chaplain..

MaLinda asked, during one of her calls to me, on 05/03/00 "Why did you call Saturday and call me a slut?" (I did not do this).

Concerns:

- Question about my car I had or have.
- How and when do I get my kids?
- As of 04/26/00, I was suspended without pay from work, as a teacher.

05/03/00 – I was so distraught that I was in deep prayer. on my recliner. in the living room. I believe that out of depression, later on 05/03/2000, I was so bothered by MaLinda's phone call that I called Susan, the Detective, back and told her that I would take a polygraph. Susan called back later and informed me that the polygraph test would be Friday, 05/05/00, at 8:00 A.M. I told Susan that I would be there. Susan told me that sometimes lawyers can be wrong, when I told her of the legal advice I had received concerning not to take a polygraph test.

05/04/2000 – I was about to go out of my house to go to "Teen Talk" when the phone rang at 4:40 p.m. The Christian Law Association (CLA) was on the phone with the names of two more attorneys: The CLA gave me the phone numbers to their offices. I immediately called one of the attorneys. The attorney received my call. I told him my situation. He informed me, under strict legal advice, not to take the polygraph test. I was under no obligation to take the polygraph – I was not arrested – something is wrong here – they apparently do not have anything on me or I would not be talking to him. I questioned him concerning my possibility of being arrested. He told me to go and do my radio program, but that I was not to take the polygraph test. He mentioned about nervousness – false positive results – and probable cause the test might give them reason to arrest me for something that I had not done. I thanked him and took his conversation as an answer of God's protection. With that, I went to do the "Teen Talk" program.

About 9:40 p.m. on 05/04/00, I called and left a message on Susan Kirkland's answering machine at her office that I would not be in to take the polygraph test Friday at 8 AM. I had received strict legal advise..

05/05/00 (Friday) at 8:00 a.m.–Susan Kirkland called me at my house and said that "David, you're late for the polygraph test." I reiterated my message to her office answering machine at 9:40 p.m. 05/04/00. She told me alright and hung up.

05/05/00 – 2 p.m. (I really do not remember the exact time). I was again in deep prayer and asking for God's help for my situation, when I heard my name being called from my back-yard. It was Susan Kirkland and Earl Fisher, the detectives. While looking in my small fish pond, Earl asked how I was. Then Earl said to Susan, "Are you ready to give him the bad news?" With that, Susan said that I was being arrested for tampering with a witness. They handcuffed me and did not allow me to call anyone. They did not read me my rights. However, they did shut my windows, turn off my TV, and locked my doors. Earl had his car. He said that he could not transport me to the jail in his car. They took me downtown where we sat outside the Sheriff's Office until an officially marked sheriff's car came to transport me to jail. The wait was about five minutes, I believe.

******

Chapter VIII

JAIL TIME (CONTINUED)

I did not speak to the deputy, on the way, to the county jail. I knew where the jail was, because I traveled that same country road every Thursday evening to conduct a Bible study. with incarcerated male youth. The Bible study was sponsored by the County's chaplain.

We got to the jail. We did not go through the front door. as was my custom, when I came for the Bible study. Instead, the deputy drove the car around to the back, pulled in front of a huge metal garage door, put his window down and pressed the call button and announced that I was arriving at the jail. The large garage door rolled open and the deputy pulled into the back of the jail. The garage door was then closed. Another deputy opened the back passenger door of the car and told me to "get out!" I slid across the back seat. With every move, the handcuffs got tighter. The deputy helped me stand up and told me to enter a bolted door where I was un-handcuffed, told to strip, and to put all my belongings in a large zip-lock bag. The deputy took the inventory. My eyes were too blurred. I couldn't care less about my belongings. I wanted to "wake up" and go home.

Next, they gave me a shower and asked me my clothing and shoe size. I went from window to window to receive the clothing, shoes, blanket (sheet), and toiletries. I was told to get dressed, in my new jail clothing. On top of the pile of items that I had, they placed the required rules and regulations. I do not remember this, but upon entry, they took my fingerprints, mug shot, personal information, and I was examined by a medical professional and asked about my medical history.

Amidst cat calls and whistles, I was walked to my cell. Then the deputy left.

The cell had two sets of bunkbeds, a toilet, and a sink connected to the toilet. No doors in the toilet area. The cell was stark, usual government gray floor and cream colored walls. The bunkbeds were made of iron with metal chain springs. The mattress was about 4" thick, easy to fold in half and carry.

As I entered the cell, I noticed that only the one bunkbed, the one up against the right wall was fully taken, so I proceeded to attempt to put my things on the lower bunkbed, on the left wall. All of a sudden, another inmate threw his stuff on the lower bed and said, "This is my bed. If you want it, you've got to fight me. You chicken lover!" (I took that to mean, I guess word was out as to why I was in). I did not feel like fighting, so I quickly threw my items on the top bunk. The inmate stated, "Learnin' already." He spat at my feet.

I jumped up onto the top bunk and let my feet dangle over the side of the bed. There was a narrow, long window at the foot of the bed. I looked out of the window and saw cows grazing, in the field, behind the jail. The sheriff grew a lot of fresh vegetables and had cows, which supplied milk for us, the inmates. I got very angry and spewed out of my mouth, "God damn it! Those cows are free and I'm not!" All of a sudden, there was a loud roar of thunder. Everyone got still. But I heard, "I will never leave you nor forsake you!" Whispers throughout the pod were words such as, "What was that?" "Where did that thunder come from?" Only I heard the words, which I believe to this day was God letting me know that He was still in charge.

"I've got to find me a Bible," I thought.

So I jumped down from the top bunk, headed out of the cell, went to the little enclosed room to my left, and opened the door. I saw four inmates sitting with their Bibles opened and the lead inmate Bible teacher holding a Gideon's red Bible up in the air, with his right hand. Everyone in the small room stopped and stared at me. I recognized all five inmates. All used to come to my Bible studies that I held every Thursday evening sponsored by the sheriff's department chaplain. (I was a volunteer for the chaplain). Finally, the lead inmate Bible teacher said, "Pastor Dave, what are you doing in here?" (Back when I was a volunteer for the Chaplain, the inmates called me "Pastor Dave.")

I answered, "Never mind why I am in here. I want to know why there are so few of you in here for Bible study?"

With that stated, I grabbed the leader's Bible, which I have to this day, and proceeded to go out to the pod area, to tell the others that it was Bible study time. Out of the 50+ inmates in the pod, I knew most of them. They used to come to my Bible studies when I was a volunteer. I got about 26 guys to come into the room.

As the Bible study leader was about to begin, one of the inmates whom I knew, when he was only 15 years old, asked me if I remembered the last time that he was in my Bible study group at the jail when he was 15 years old? I stated that I remembered him, but did not remember what I had said. He answered, "You promised to read I Corinthians 13. Would you please read it to all of us now?" Then he said something that really shocked me. "And he said, my pants are pulled up!" Everyone laughed. You see, when I went to the juvenile part of the jail, all the boys came. I had a rule which was, when you come to Bible study, all pants had to be pulled up. We were there to compare and study the Bible, not underwear or butts. This inmate remembered this rule. At the time of my incarceration, he was 19 years old.

The Bible study leader gave me permission to read I Corinthians 13. All listened intently. Praise The Lord (PTL)!

At the conclusion of the Bible study, we got on our knees and all had the opprutunity to pray, Finally, it was bedtime and lights out.

In the late afternoon, every day I would conduct an exercise class. An average of 10 inmates would gather in and outside of my cell. No officer ever stopped us from gathering. The regulations stated that no more than four inmates could gather in or around a cell, at one time. This class continued as long as I was in jail. I taught the guys isometric and kinesthetic exercises. We had timed events to see who could do the most push-ups in one minute. Another timed event was to stand with your back to the wall and slide down to a sitting position. We wanted to see who could stay in the seated position for the longest time. This exercise made your quadriceps and upper leg muscles burn and develop. The guys made sure that I held the class every evening, during unlock time.

It was during one of these sessions that a young inmate pulled me aside and asked me if he could have what kept me happy, even in my situation. (At this time, he had heard the news on TV and in thelocal newspaper, about my allegations). I had the opportunity to share the Gospel of Jesus Christ with him. At the end of our discussing, he bowed his head and accepted Jesus as his Savior and friend. When he lifted his head from the prayer, which he said in his own words, he announced to the whole pod, "I have Jesus!" One of the guards picked up the microphone and said, "Amen!" Wonder where this man is now? Say a prayer for him please.

****

Chapter IX

OFFICER"S LATE NIGHT VISIT

One night around midnight, I was asleep. I heard my name being called from outside of the cell, and a bright light was shining in my eyes.

"David, get up and follow me!" the officer demanded. So, I got down from my bunk, put on my jail shoes, and went toward the gate. The deputy opened the gate very quietly and said, "Follow me, we're going to the clinic."

I thought, "Oh no, they want more blood."

While crossing the pod, there were cat calls such as "Officer got his boy!" "Hey pretty boy, save some for me!" The officer told me to ignore their calls.

We entered the clinic. The officer turned on the light. I looked at him and remembered thinking, "I've seen him before." The officer told me to sit down and pointed to a chair. He sat across from me. He asked, "Do you recognize me?" I told him that I remember that he was one of the guards that used to let me in and out of the juvenile part of the jail, when I came

Thursday evenings for mimistry. He nodded. Then he asked, "Do you know why I brought you here?"

I said, "You want more blood from me?"

He shook his head and said, "You of all people should not be in here for the reason you are being accused." "I brought you here to tell you that you saved my life and my marriage."

"I did?" I asked. "How?"

He told me his story as follows: "One Thursday evening, about a month ago, I decided to come into the room to hear what you were telling the boys. They were all listening so intently and respectfully; so, I began listening. You were reading from the Bible about the story of St. Paul's conversion. You made it pertinent and understandable. When you asked the boys if anyone wanted to ask Jesus into their heart and life, just speak out and say, "Yes." A few of them said, "Yes." Then, you did something that I never saw done before. You asked everyone to bow their heads and close their eyes. You asked the boys who said yes, to take a stand and just let Jesus know that they believe and invite Jesus into their heart and life, in their own words. You didn't tell them what to say, and by golly, each boy prayed their own prayer, in their own words, and in their own street jargon. I want to tell you, Pastor Dave, I was one of those "boys," except I whispered my own prayer, because I did not want to interrupt. You see, Pastor Dave, my life was a mess. My wife and I were about to get a divorce. I couldn't wait to get home, to my wife, and share what had happened, in the jail that Thursday evening. I shared with her, from the Bible, of St. Paul's conversion. Don't know if it was as good as you did, but when I finished, I asked if she wanted to ask

Jesus into her heart and life. She said, "Yes." I told her to bow her head, close her eyes, and in her own words, ask Jesus into her heart and life. She prayed a beautiful, simple prayer. Afterward, we kissed, and we've been kissing ever since. My wife is now expecting. So, Pastor Dave, thank you."

I remarked, "No, not me, praise God."

Then the deputy asked, "Do you need anything?"

I laughed, "Yes, get me out of here!"

He laughed and said, "Can't do that, but do you need anything else?"

"Yes," I answered, "more blankets. It's cold in here and my asthma acts up. I'm right across from the air conditioning vent."

With that, the deputy stood up, turned around, went into the closet in the clinic and brought out seven sheets and handed them to me.

"Blankets are not allowed in the jail, and you are only allowed one sheet." "Here, cover up with these. Hand in only one sheet per day and rotate the sheets. Please, turn in only one sheet per day." I agreed that I understood. "If you get caught," he said, "I'll take the blame." Use all sheets to cover youself, during the night, "Anything else?"

"No," I said. I thanked him.

"I see your cell mate, on the top bunk, has covered the air conditioner vent. Was that for you?"

"Yes," I answered.

"He told me that he heard me wheezing and he didn't want "Pastor Dave" to get sick. The inmates needed me for exercise class and daily Bible study." "I see nothing," stated the deputy.

"Just ask him to take it down right after reveille, at 5 a.m." I said that I would.

With that, the deputy walked me back across the pod. Again, there were cat calls, "Get what you wanted deputy?" The deputy opened my cell gate, said "Goodnight and thanks again, Pastor Dave."

I whispered back, "Thank you, Sir."

The night got quiet, and I was warm! The hand of my Heavenly Father was at work, in my life.

****

Chapter X

OUT, BUT NOT FREE

I do not remember the date the following happened, but I remember it was a Tuesday in May 2000. It was about 10 a.m. During "out time" (out of cell time in jail). I was outside in the basketball caged, in court area, shooting hoops with an inmate I'll call "Big Jim." Big Jim was about 6 feet 7 inches tall and weighed about 260 pounds. I was only 5 feet 8 inches and weighed about 160 pounds. So, to keep the game fair, we played either pig or horse. Those are games where the player stands in one spot anywhere on the court, shoots the ball, and scores a letter if he makes the shot. The first player to spell the word pig or horse wins. The game was fair that way because, when we played one on one, Big Jim creamed me.

This morning, Big Jim and I were playing. I said to Big Jim, "You know, I just feel my time is up in here and I am getting out today."

Big Jim smiled, laughed, and said, "How'd ya know? God tell you or somethin?"

I told Big Jim that I don't know. I just feel it. I think God needs me out of here to help on the outside.

We continued to play, within a few minutes after our conversation, my name was called over the loud speaker. "David Jonathan, please report to the guard's desk immediately!"

Big Jim laughed and said, "Either you're gone or you did something wrong." Then I thought of the sheets I had. I made my way to the guard's desk. "David Jonathan reporting, Sir."

"Here is a basket and a clothing bag. Get dressed. You've been bailed out." I grabbed the basket and bag, ran out to the basketball court and shouted out to Big Jim, "Hey Big Jim, I'm outta here." "No!" shouted Big Jim, "You can't go Pastor Dave. We all need you in here!"

"That may be, Big Jim, but God apparently wants me out there. My work in here is done. You'll have to carry on, Big Jim! You know how to pray and do Bible study."

Big Jim dropped the basketball, ran over to me, and with tears in his eyes, he said, "Sure gonna miss you, Pastor Dave." He gave me a big hug and said, "No, go on, get outa here. Just keep prayin for us in here, and we will keep prayin for ya out there. We gonna miss ya!"

I thanked Big Jim, gave him a big shoulder hug and promised I would keep praying for all the guys and him in there. With that, I quickly went back to my cell to collect my things. I still have the Bible that I got from the jail, on my first day, in jail. I still pray for Big Jim and the guys. Big Jim was awaiting his transfer to prison. He killed someone with a knife. Never knew his real name, so I could not stay in contact with him, but God can through my prayers.

I gave my jail items to the guard. He, in turn, gave me my personal items that I came with to the jail. He told me to check my things to make sure they were all there. Everything was there, except my money. I informed the guard about the missing money.

He said, "Oh yes. Remember when you had a headache and you were given two Tylenol?"

I said, "Yes, I remember."

He told me, "Well the two Tylenol cost the amount of money you had in your wallet."

I did not respond; however, I thought, $28 for two Tylenol?" I just wanted out, so I moved on to the next checkout station. I had no idea what or who put up my bond money. Also, I had no idea who was going to pick me up and take me home.

The last jail house door unlocked and opened up. I stepped out into the main lobby of the jail. The door slid shut and locked behind me. I was free! I mentioned that to the guard in the lobby. He said, "Yes, but don't leave the county, at least for the next few months." I was told that I would have to ask permission if I wanted to leave the county. I was given the information and phone number to call.

Then, I heard my name being called out by someone in the lobby. I turned around. It was Rob, a friend since we were in junior high school. I said, "Rob?" Rob said, "Come one stupid, follow me." I followed Rob to the car. We didn't say a word. He started toward my house. It felt great to be free, for now I thought. About 10 minutes into the ride home, Rob said, "You're lucky to be out today." (It was Friday). I asked, "Why?" "Well," Rob answered, "the bondsman was on his way for a two-week vacation. Nobody knew this." I wanted to know who the "nobodies" were. He told me that the community raised $1000 for my bail. Rob and his wife put their house up for collateral against the $10,000 bond. So, Rob stated, "You ain't goin' nowhere, but to your house." He went on to explain that he lived about 20 miles south from the bondsman and the other lady who had the last $100 lived about 30 miles north of the bondsman. No one called ahead to make sure the bondsman was at his office. Unknowingly to each other, they both headed toward the bondsman. In the meantime, the bondsman left for his two-week vacation, but he forgot some papers at his office, so he turned around and headed back. All three of them, Rob, the lady, and the bondsman pulled up to the office, at the same time. The bondsman took care of the bail money and gave Rob and the lady a receipt to take to the jail for my release. (Wow! Talk about God moving!) "So," Rob continued, "You are lucky to be out, stupid."

"Why do you keep calling me stupid" I asked?

"I'll tell you when we get to your house." I was taken aback by Rob's name calling, so we did not speak for the rest of the way home. We pulled into my dirt driveway, got out of the car and went inside. The house was hot and muggy. Rob sat on the couch. I turned on the air conditioning, then sat in the Lazy boy chair across from him. "Gee, it felt good to be home," I thought.

"So," I said, "why am I stupid?"

"Well, for one thing, you have no savings, and you spent your money on TV and radio programs with kids, and look where it's got you!"

"But I was helping kids to be successful!"

And Rob stated, "Look where you are. No money. No job. A wrecked car. How you gonna live?"

"I guess I'll just have to let that up to God."

Rob snickered. "Well, guess you're gonna have to. My wife and I have helped you all we can. So, don't ask us for money. You know you'll need a lawyer. They ain't cheap."

To tell the truth, I never thought of getting a lawyer. Rob was right. "God will have to handle and direct me to get me a lawyer."

"Well, stupid, I'm outta here. Keep in touch." I said that I would. "You still have a phone," Rob asked? "Did you pay 'that' bill?"

I lifted up the land line phone and heard a dial tone. "Must have," I said. "It's still working." I could not remember the last time I had paid the phone bill.

"Ok," Rob called out, "See ya! Stay in touch."

I waved goodbye to Rob as he backed out of my driveway, and headed back, to his home. I closed and locked the door; then, fell to my knees sobbing. "Oh God," I prayed through my sobs, "Remember what you told me in jail that you would never leave me nor forsake me? Please don't forget about me now! For Jesus' sake."

I got up from my knees, went to the bedroom, and flopped down on my bed. I sobbed myself to sleep. What have I done?

When I woke up, it was dark. I got out of bed to go to the bathroom. I remembered how good it felt to be home, in my own bed, and have the privacy of my bathroom. I went to the refrigerator and got myself a cool glass of water. This water was in a clean glass, unlike the jail. Never knew what somebody might do to your cup in jail.

I went back to bed. It was around 10 p.m. My mind became flooded with the following: Maybe Rob is right. Maybe I am stupid. Where am I going to get money to get food, pay the rent, and pay the bills? Where will I get the money for a lawyer? How am I going to live? What if I get sick? I threw all of these questions at God. Then I yelled, "Why me God?! What have I done!" Again, I cried myself back into a deep sleep.

I was 51 years old. Alone. No money. No one. Now, accused of something I did not do! What is happening in my life? I was awakened by someone knocking on the backdoor and calling my name in a loud whisper, "Mr. Jonathan! Mr. Jonathan! Are you home?" The person wriggled the door handle. Thank God the door was locked. I heard the car running in the driveway. The car's lights lit up the back yard. I froze in bed and pulled the covers up over my head. Quietly, I called out to God. "God, what's happening? Are the police back to get me again? Oh God, help me please!" The calling and knocking went on for about 10 minutes. It seemed like an eternity. Then the person walked around to the bathroom, knocked on the window and loudly whispered my name several times. I didn't budge. Next, I heard the back gate open and close. The car sped out of the driveway. I remember thinking that at least they did not try a forced entry.

Oh no! The car is back! The person left the car running and lights on. I heard the car door open. The back gate opened and slammed shut. The person opened the screen door, then closed it. I heard the back gate open and slammed shut. The car door was closed and the car sped out of the driveway. The person was gone, at least for now. What did they want? Who was the person? "Oh God, please help me!" I did not get out of bed. I stayed under the covers crying out to God. What have I done?! Why me?!

****

Answered prayer

I woke up the next morning and went to the back door. I opened the door and taped, to the window, was an envelope with my name on it. I opened the envelope and there was twenty-five $20 bills totalling $500.00! It was from a school board member. He stopped by my house later that day to see if I was okay, and I had gotten the money. He prayed with me; then, he left.

Chapter XI

A MAN'S CRY

(Written July 1, 2000 – 4:17 p.m.)

A man is crying. Is that you? Go ahead; God loves your tears. Jesus wept. Tears wash the heart's strings and make then soft and clean, for God's hands to turn the crying into sounds of rejoicing for His honor. Tears become showers of blessing. Tears of gladness in desperate hope of repentance. What did I do?

Go ahead, man cry. Cry real tears. Shed the burden. Clean out your heart. Let God provide the streams of water in your desert life, because real men love Jesus. I cried out to God, and He heard me. My life feels like a coin without value. But with Jesus, God's Love, when I am nothing, He, and He alone, makes me something: A jewel for His crown filled with the Spirit of His Word, His love, and God's tears of joy!

Go ahead, man cry. It's good for the soul. God, when you let Him, He will turn your tears into joy so that you can look at others; see their pain, see their hurt, and lead them to the Savior, who shed tears for them. So, go head man, cry. It does a body good. It melts the heart of stone and shows that you are human. Though weak, God will provide the strength for you to march onward, through the blur of tears into His arms of love and mercy. He has to guide a tearful man, because life is too blurred. He will! Let God have His way, and go ahead man, cry. See God's love!

Experience God's strength in your weakness. In weakness, there is a well of strength. In tears, there is a cleansing power.

So, go ahead, man, cry. Cry for your soul. Cry for God's mercy; then cry for the lost. Through your tears, others will see Jesus, God's Living Word. God's true love! So, go ahead man, cry.

(2 Peter 3:17-18)

(Psalms 8:9)

****

Chapter XII

EPISODE

Miracles from God – By Faith
How God Leads Without My Moving

On 05/26/2000, I received a return phone call from Pete at Christian Law Assdciation (CLA). We talked for quite a while. He told me of a similar case of a P. Scott. He did not have his email address; nor did he give me P. Scott's home address. He did give me the name of P. Scott's lawyers, who were helping him pro-bono. I took down P. Scott's name and the Orlando attorney that was helping him.

I do not remember what time I called Rob and Mandy, but I asked if I could spend the weekend at their house. They said, "Yes." And so, I planned to leave Saturday morning.

Sunday, I got on their computer and tried to find P. Scott. I emailed Marie; then, wrote a letter to P. Scott online, concerning my case. I literally blindly sent it out to a P. Scott. I remember that I could not find the name of his attorney online. I left it at that. I checked later ,to see if a P. Scott responded to my e-mail. It was about 4 p.m., Sunday, P. Scott had not responded.

Monday, 05/29/2000, I spent a great deal of time praying and reading the Bible and a book. I asked God for a miracle. I was thinking about someone calling me to "help" me. A few people did call. A few kids called to talk and pray with me. I encouraged them, and God, through them, encouraged me. I thanked God for their calls. I cried a little, because I thought Mandy and Rob and the rest of my "friends" didn't want to spend the Memorial Day holiday with me: a criminal. I was lonely, but I knew with Jesus Christ, I was not alone. I thought of the guys in jail and thanked God that I was out and able to enjoy my home. I gave all my things in this house back to God. I thanked Him for the miracles he performed in my life thus far through this situation: The raising of my bond of $1000 and the money he supplied, to me, for the much needed lawyers, who stood by me even, when I was in jail, before I hired them! I had no money, but God did and He, in His own loving, merciful way, helped to hire my attorneys..

Rob kept telling me that "God helps those who help themselves"; yet, while I was imprisoned, God was working, without my headstrong will and ideas. God was mysteriously, mercifully, and lovingly moving, without my help, to help me! I was helpless. I was behind bars! God was not! I kept reading in the Bible to "wait on the Lord"; so, in jail, all I could do was wait on Him. Even now, God know the gospel seed that was sown, through Him bringing me into the lives of many people. They are watching to see if God is all powerful, and to see, if by faith, they can trust God to perform, in His time and in His way, for my life.. I am not a perfect man. I am a forgiven man, from all my past. God knows the falsity of my present situation. God knows that I have asked Him to forgive her. He knows that I do not want to act hastily out of desperation, to try to run ahead of His will and His way in my life. He leads me. His Word is a lamp unto my path and a light unto my pathway. His Word is living and powerful. He will renew my strength, and be mounted up with wings like eagles. I shall run and not be weary. I shall walk and not faint. When I wait on the Lord. I prayerfully move and act on the things and people God brings into my life. I am learning to act through and by faith on God's actions – not on my own. He knows the hardest thing for me to do is to wait and not act on my own intellectual ideas and thoughts. God is teaching me, because now I am willing to be willing to quietly wait. I have no resource to act with unless, He makes the way. I am broke and broken. God is not broke, nor is He broken. God is all powerful. He needs me to be His ambassador – to carry out what He has done and will do to all those who walk, including myself, according to His purpose and not my purpose. My only action right now is faithful prayer, asking for God's mercy, and for Him to show His love to this humble, meek, and waiting servant. What a lesson to learn. And, as David, the Psalmist, I am to behave myself wisely in all that I say and do.

"Oh Heavenly Father, your wish is my command. I can do nothing. I am weak, but you, Oh Father, you alone are strong. You are my strong refuge and defense. God, you know my broken heart – broken will. I am willing even to sell what I have, if it is your will. If it is your will and purpose, you, Heavenly

Father, will make a way. I must wait. I must trust. I must obey. You will make a way as you have, in and through my life, down here. Thank you, Father God."

****

Chapter XIII

"Miracles from God"

I did get an attorney. I drove up to Clearwater, FL on a Wednesday. The attorney told me that he would take my case, but it would cost me $6000.00. I told him that I was broke. He stood up, shook my hand, and wished me good luck.

All the way home, I was in tears and praying for a miracle.

I got home and went straight to bed. Then, it all started. People came by with food, money, and prayers. This continued all through Thursday, so by Thursday evening, I had $6,205.00! I put the money in my Bible and slept with it.

Friday morning, I woke up around 5 a.m., got ready, and drove the 2-1/2-hour drive to Clearwater, FL. I was sitting on the attorney's door steps when he arrived for work. He saw me and said, "David, what are you doing here?" I told him that I came to hire him. He said, "But I thought you didn't have any money?"

I said, "I do now. Let's go into your office."

When we got into his office, I quickly opened my Bible and took out the money and notes people gave to me. The attorney remarked over and over again, "Unbelievable!" He stood up, shook my hand, and said, "Let's get started." After signing all the paperwork, he told me that he would take it from there.

I spent the summer of 2000 working at odd jobs, cutting grass, washing cars, painting rooms and houses, to name a few. Never missed a rent or bill payment. No one would hire me for a regular job.

I got discouraged, so I boxed up all my antiques, including my Persian rugs, and rented two spaces, at the local flea market. People came by and just walked through. Nothing sold Friday evening, all day Saturday, or Sunday afternoon. I called my mother and told her what I did and that nothing sold. She said, "David, looks like God wants you to keep them. Pack them up and take them back to your house." So, I did. I did not unpack them.

I received a phone call, from a doctor friend. He told me that his friend had a job opening as a Behavior Specialist. The doctor friend and his wife told the employer about my situation, but that I was a good man and great Behavior Specialist. I had previously worked with their son, who had behavior issues. The doctor friend of mine asked if he could give the employer my phone number, and would I talk with the employer. I said that he could give the employer my phone number. This was around the middle of August 2000. My case was still ongoing, according, to my lawyer. I was a nervous wreck not knowing if the deputies would surround my house and pick me up again.

The medics did come out to my house with the two original detectives to draw more blood for testing. They drew the blood from my right arm right out in the middle of the yard, for all to see. Yes, this happened to me right here in America!

I called my lawyer, and he told me that the fact I am still at my house and that they released me. on bond, meant that the sheriff had no evidence. on me. My lawyer stated that the sheriff better have had a search warrant. He would check into this. The sheriff's office did not inform him nor me about needing more blood tests.

My lawyer stated that he had not received anything from the State's Attorney's Office as of the middle of August 2000.

06/06/2000:

I woke up at 7:02 a.m. This is one of those days that I feel apprehensive. God forgive me. I feel that something is going to happen today. I find myself afraid to walk around in my house because "they are spying on me." Lord forgive me for this feeling. Deep down there is a voice that is saying, "David, I will protect you through this." I will never leave you nor forsake you." Thank you, Heavenly Father, for your faithful reassurance. After all, your reputation is on the line! So, You deal with today, as you have, in the past. I'll let go. I'm snuggled in your arms for another day. Together, we can handle the events of today, God willing, moment by moment. The song, "We Are Standing in His Presence" is playing over my stero speakers. Praise God, even my stereo system, the one I got in 1981, sounds clearer and sweeter this morning.

The Behavior Specialist job was in Pennsylvania. The employer said that he would send me the application and the necessary requirements for the job. "Fill everything out and send all the paperwork back to me. You sound like you are qualified. I am offering you the position pending clearance." Then we hung up.

"Oh God, I cried, please help me out of this situation!" I felt like a wild animal caged up, in my own house.

****

Chapter XIV

GOD'S VICTORY

E arly September 2000, I received a letter, from my attorney, stating that the case was abandoned/dropped and that the State's Attorney's Office will not file any charges against me. He stated that I am free now and to go on with my life. I did!

I was cleared to take the Behavior Specialist job in Pennsylvania. I would be working with Autistic children and writing their behavior treatment plans. So, I moved to Pennsylvania into a twenty-one room farmhouse! I worked from Octobr 30, 2000 until October 30, 2002. The job as a Behavior Specialist was no longer extended to me.

On October 31, 2002, I moved back to Florida. I was cleared to teach school and to work with the troubled teens in the Juvenile Justice System. Through God's infinite love and mercy, I was able to retire. June 13, 2016, to a beautiful Log Cabin home, in Crawfordville, FL. The address is Log Cabin Road. I own the road! My teaching certificate is valid through June 31, 2020. So, I can still teach, if I want to do so.

****

Conclusion

My final words, of this book, to anyone going through a similar situation or any stressful situation, are from scripture:

> "Trust in the Lord with all your heart, and do not lean on your own understanding. In all your ways acknowledge Him, and He will make your paths straight..."

New American Standard Bible
Proverbs 3:5-6
Thank you for reading Storms in Life Bring Richer Ground.
Blessings,
(my signature)
David Jonathan

STORMS IN LIFE BRING RICHER GROUND

(The Lighter Side of Life)
(A little about myself, with the following pictures, poems, letters, and awards)

The following are stories on my chilhood. I am following my advice. During the writing of this book, I had to stop, ask God for the strength to continuing writing this event, read scropture, and read pleasant memoirs from my childhood. I hope you can laugh, with me.

Memories of A Small Town Boy

1. _Childhood Story_

I remember the innocence of my youth. I will share this story. It was Valentine's Day. I believe I was in first grade. So, the year must have been about 1956. It was a very cold February day. I had a crush on a girl in my class name "Linda." It had snowed about 12 to 18 inches the day before Valentine's Day. However, after the snow, the sun came out and warmed the temperature to above freezing. This caused the snow to melt.

The temperature dropped below freezing during the evening of the 13th, and Valentine's Day was a bitter cold, wintry day. It was so cold that you could walk on top of the snow. The melted snow had refrozen. The process of the snow melting and refreezing had turned our yard into a frozen wonderland of snow and ice. The landscape looked like a sheet of frozen vanilla icing. I could walk on top of the icing and not fall through.

I remember coming home from school. I went inside my house and put my school books down. I went back outside to play in the winter wonderland of ice and snow. "I was in first grade and "deeply" i love!" I had a queasy feeling inside, and I was very quiet. I was experiencing "puppy love." I took a branch from the old apple tree and made a point out of one of the ends. I proceeded to cut hearts out of the snow "icing" in the backyard. I was cutting a Valentine for Linda, but I did not want my mother or anyone else in the family to know that I was "in love." So, I cut a heart out for my mother and brought it into the house as a Valentine's gift. Even at that early age, I was a quick thinker. I'm sure my mother has other words to express her opinion concerning some of my antics growing up.

Thanks for letting me share one my memorable times of my childhood. It is those memories that take my mind off of the reality. of the situation. I'm going through. Here's some good advice. While going through a terrible time in your life, try to think of a pleasant time, of your life, and relive that experience, either by writing about the experience, or by closing your eyes and just picturing the experience all over again. Praise the Lord for the good times. Remember one thing as a Christian: "All things work together for good to those who love God and walk according to His purpose." (Romans 8:28). Even so-called "bad times" have a purpose for good, in God's timetable. I will share more "quiet storms" of my childhood memories, with you, during the course of this book.

:)

2. Advice/Childhood Memory

Keep busy. Do not take yourself out of the mainstream of life. In other words thank God, I have not allowed myself to totally shut down. I have speaking engagements, Bible studies, go to dinners, and maintain friendships with, fortunately, lots of pretty nice folks.

Take breaks. Go outside. Do some yard work or do a fun project. Keep your mind occupied. Do not try to figure out the circumstance. Put it in God's hands. I know that too, is easier said than done. However, God's grace is sufficient throughout any storm. I can assure you of that fact. Here's an example of what I mean by keeping your mind occupied on other things.

I remember one time when I was younger. I must have been about seven or eight years old. I was raised during the time of television programs such as "Davy Crocket" and "The Lone Ranger." All of us kids loved to watch those programs because "Davy Crocket" and "The Lone Ranger" were our "heroes." Also, Saturday mornings had Western Cowboy tele-vision programs. Much like today's youth, we imitated what we saw on television. Remember, this is the 50's I'm talking about. Heroes conquered evil. Boys were boys and girls were girls.

I was playing Cowboys and Indians, with my older brother who is ten years older than me.

My older brother's friends captured me and placed me inside a hollowed out vine that had grown up around a telephone pole. They proceeded to tie me to the pole. They left me there tied to the pole to go out and look for other Indians. Did I tell you that pole was in the middle of the woods? My brother and his friends never captured another "Indian," nor did they come back to untie me. They got preoccupied with something else and left me stranded in the woods tied to the pole. It got dark, and I got scared. No matter how loudly I called for help, no one came. No one heard me! I would have to spend the night in the deep, dark woods tied to the pole.

As time passed, I remember making up my mind that I would probably have to spend the night alone in the woods with my hands tied. You know, I cannot remember whether or not I had to go to the bathroom, but I do not think I did. That would not be the case today. Of course, I am about forty-three years older, and my kidneys are not what they used to be. At the age, my only worry was that a bear or snake would come and get me. I camped out a lot, when I was younger, so being outside at night was nothing new. I was a nature boy at heart.

Finally, my brother and his friends noticed that I was nowhere to be found. They finally missed me! (At least in the 1950s, you were a lot safer in the woods than you would be today). They ran to rescue me. My brother knew he was in trouble. I have to admit that I was scared, but I knew eventually someone would miss me and come looking for me. At least it was a warm evening.

I was told that my parents had called our town's only cop. Everybody was out looking for me with flashlights. My brother was afraid to tell our parents where I was. So he quickly hurried to the spot, untied me, and brought me home. I was safe and sound in the house, but my brother was not. He got into trouble. I tried to explain to my mom and dad that it was no big deal, but to them it was. Now that I am older, I agree. It was funny then, but looking back on that situation, I can laugh about it now. I was covered with insect bites. But I survived! And I am left with a fond childhood memory.

That's just like this storm. I may be covered with "insect bites" from being out in the trenches of the storm, but with God's help I will survive. Remember, He is the God who can calm any storm, at any time, in His time. The clouds will pass. The sun will shine again in my life. I do not believe I will laugh. at this storm. I will just praise God for caring for me all the way through the storm! What is the old saying, "Back of the clouds, the sun is always shining." With my God, the Son is always shining!

Didn't you get a chuckle out of that story? See what I mean about occupying your mind with more pleasant thoughts? Read a Psalm or two. Talk to God in prayer.

:)

3. Sadie: "The Witch"

She was walking down the middle of the road all hunched over and dragging a huge tree branch behind her. "Quick, come look at the witch!" I shouted.

Everyone came running out onto the porch to stare. Her name was Sadie. We called her "Sadie the Witch." We just knew that she had magical powers and cast voodoo spells. Sadie was old. Her hair was pulled back tightly into a small, brush-like pony tail. Her face showed the scars of many hurtful years. She had wrinkled tough turkey-like skin, and her bowed legs and bony fingers were crippled with arthritis.

She never spoke much to anyone. She would work alone for many hours in her vegetable garden, which she plowed, tilled, and planted all by hand. No one in the town ever spoke to her. I remember watching her work in the hot, humid dog days of summer and feeling sorry for her, but you didn't talk to Sadie lest she cast an evil spell on you."

Early one August morning, I was coming downstairs to have a bowl of cereal. No one in the house was awake. As I was walking through the dining room, I heard a noise on the back porch. I lifted a slat on the Venetian blind to look out the window. I saw Sadie the Witch walking off the porch and out of our yard! I froze. She must have cast a spell on our house! Then, I thought, no, maybe she slept on the porch or maybe she was hungry and wanted something to eat.

I waited until she walked out of sight; then, I carefully opened the porch door. At the foot of the door lay a brown paper bag. Oh no, I thought, Sadie left a curse on our house in the bag! At that point I didn't care who was sleeping and who was not.

"Mommy! Mommy! I yelled as I dashed through the dining room and up the stairs. "Sadie the Witch left a curse on the back porch and it's alive. It's got hair on it 'cause the hair is sticking out of the brown bag!"

There was no stopping them. Down the stairs my brothers, sisters and mom rushing as if a bat had escaped and come down from the attic.

"There! Right there in that brown bag. I saw her. She came right up and placed the bag herself! She even looked at me with her evil eyes!" (I had to stretch the truth a little).

Mom opened the door, stooped down and picked up the bag. She looked inside.

"David, someday your imagination's gonna get you in trouble."

Mom proceeded to carefully dump the contents on the dining room table. Out came the biggest ears of corn that I had ever seen. There were nine ears, one for each of us.

"Hmm", I thought. A tear came to my eye to think that Sadie had toiled so hard and she was so poor to give away the fruits of her labor.

What really was confusing to me, was how can a mean looking old witch have a kind streak in her. Must have been because it was not Halloween.

:)

EPILOG
A Praise to God

When I think of God's great goodness,
I am reminded of his grace.
It is all sufficient full and free,
The cross of Christ, that old rugged tree.

Oh, if mankind would praise the LORD,
Like the birds in the background do.
Oh, how the earth would resound in song!
The human voice as one blended song!

One day, when He comes in power.
Then, ever knee will bow.
Oh Father, thou hast heard my crying,
And turned my mourning into dancing!

Psalms 30
2/8/2005, at Six Mile Cypress Slough, Florida 12:26 PM.
BY: David Jonathan

So, who is the wiser?

Mankind, or those turtles?

Turtles rule God in.

Mankind rules God out.

I vote for the turtles!

02/08/2005 ~ 1:50 PM

I am reminded of Job. As my heart worships and thanks the Lord of Heaven and earth for all that He has done.

> "Then Job answered the Lord, and said, " I know that thou canst do all things, and that there is no thought hid from thee. Who is he that hideth counsel without knowledge? therefore have I spoken that I understood not, even things too wonderful for me, which I knew not."
>
> 17: "So, Job died, being old, and full of days". (Job 42:1-3 & 17 1599 Geneva Bible)
>
> Amen

Fax Memo

08/10/00
1:43 p.m.
TO: Mark Fromang, P.A.
FROM: David Jonathan
RE: My case

Here we go again, Mark. Don't forget, I'm a writer. Each public official takes the oath to protect and defend the Constitution of the United States, right? If the public servant does not defend the Constitution, isn't that called treason?

When I was in high school, we studied the Constitution. I don't believe the rights endowed by our Creator have changed. The Constitution gives me the right to life, liberty, and the pursuit of happiness. It also protects me from tyranny of the government. In other words, we (me) the people are to be the watchdog of our public servants (government officials), and it is not to be the other way around. I should not have to live in the fear that I am now being forced to live in. They are to be my servants. Since when did the servant become the master over the master (we), me the people? If the public servant tries to dispute this fact, they are not defending the Constitution. The detectives, of the County Sheriff's Department, are the criminals, not me.

There are many people truly upset with the way I am being treated. There must be – there is – protection under the Constitution of the United States to protect me and restore me to the right to life, liberty, and the pursuit of happiness once again.

If I was to be fired from my job, it should have been at the beginning of this case. I basically should not have been suspended without pay in the first place. Mark, where is my protection rights under the Constitution of the United States? What happened to America since I went to school? Maybe Florida's Constitution is unconstitutional to the law of the land.

I appreciate you. I have been violated by the public servants who swore to protect my rights under the Constitution of the United States. Let's go that route.

Thank you, you know I'll keep sending you my thoughts and ideas. My prayers are with you. How did I lose my rights? Am I not still protected?

God bless you,
David Jonathan

Thank you for your commitment to community service. Through your generosity and hard work, you have shown that the tradition of neighbor helping neighbor is alive and well in our country. Your efforts profoundly influence the life of your community and they are a shining example for us all. Barbara joins me in saluting you and sending you our best wishes. God bless you.

Geo. Bush

Me: 1952

5th Grade

Education Helps, Inc.

PRESENTS:

TEEN TALK

The First Thursday of Every Month

6-7 P.M.

Only on WWPR 1490 AM

A Forum for Teen Issues and Biblical Discussion

For more information please call Education Helps, Inc. at 941-747-1991

Bible Brunch - Every Sunday 1-2pm

Brought to you by:

Molter Termite & Pest Control
941-747-8525 or 941-746-5500

Jarvis Construction - Cindy & Joel Jarvis
941-722-2500

Education Helps, Inc.

2 Chronicles 15:12- And they entered into a covenant to seek the Lord God of their fathers with all their heart and all their soul

PRESENTS:

BIBLE BRUNCH

Every Sunday-Live

2 - 3 ▓ P.M.

Only on WWPR 1490 A.M.

A forum for Biblical Discussion

Youth Produced and Directed

Live radio call in
941-745-1490

Teen Helpline:
1-800-661-2839

Live radio call in
941-745-1490

Teen Helpline:
1-800-661-2839

For more information please call Education Helps, Inc. at 941-747-1991

Also: Teen Talk- 1st Thursday of every month 6-7 P.M.

Brought to you by:
Education Helps, Inc.
· Teen Helpline: 1-800-661-2839   Home Office: 941-747-1991

The University of South Florida

*Manatee/Sarasota Alumni Chapter
and the Community Leadership Council*

Recognize

David Jonathan

as an honored

Distinguished Alumni Award Nominee

Presented May 7, 1998

Chairman, CLC
Community Affairs Committee

President, USF Manatee-
Sarasota Alumni Chapter

USF at Sarasota-Manatee
Dean and Executive Officer

Manatee Baptist Church
1501 7th Avenue East
Bradenton, Florida 34208
748-2339

Pastor Al Gill

June 18, 1998

To Whom it may concern,

David Jonathan is a gifted communicator and has been of great
service to us here at Manatee Baptist Church.
His presence in the Youth department of our Sunday School as well as in
our discipleship programs, has been a great blessing to all.
He has served the Lord, as well as us, in his duties as a youth worker.
I am looking forward to working with David, as he leads the youth in
our upcoming Billy Graham Crusade, this fall, October 22 - 25 in
Tampa, Florida.
His compassionate love for teenagers is obvious to anyone who observes
him, even if only for a brief moment.
He has consistently reached out to all and seems to be, especially
gifted in working with teenagers from dysfunctional families.
He has gone above and beyond in his effort to be a help to all who
would let him.

Cordially yours,

Alton A. Gill

Alton A. Gill, Pastor

P.S.
If I can be of further assistance to you, please feel free to call me at
the church or my home (750-8480).

MULBERRY CORPORATION

Mulberry Phosphates, Inc. · Piney Point Phosphates, Inc. · Nu-Gulf Industries, Inc.

June 21, 1999

Mr. David Jonathan
601 - 45th Street West
Bradenton, FL 34209

Dear Mr. Jonathan,

The Mulberry Corporation employees wish to express their congratulations to you for your nomination as a 1999 University of South Florida Distinguished Alumni. Your professional achievement and community involvement have contributed to the enhancement of USF and its legacy.

Thank you for your commitment to the Sarasota-Manatee area and its future.

Sincerely,

Marcie Lipscomb

Marcie Lipscomb
Public Communications Manager

To Whom It May Concern;

I have known David Jonathan for two years. During this time David has been a positive influence in my life. I have seen his involvement with some of the young people in this area and have participated on one of their radio talk shows and observed the caring attitude and respect these young people have for him, and he for them. I trust David completely as friend, a prayer partner, and an influential person in our church and community. I am grateful to have known him.

Sincerely,

Kimberly Mitchell-Henry

THE FLORIDA SENATE

Tallahassee, Florida 32399-1100

COMMITTEES:
Rules and Calendar,
  Chairman
Agriculture and Consumer Services
Children and Families
Commerce and Economic Opportunities
Fiscal Resource
Gubernatorial Appointments and Confirmations

SENATOR JOHN MCKAY
26th District

March 2, 2000

To Whom It May Concern:

It is with pleasure that I offer my recommendation of Mr. David Jonathan.

I have known David for many years and can attest to his honesty and strength of character. His dedication to helping emotionally troubled youth succeed in life resulted in *Education Helps, Inc.*, a non-profit organization offering a variety of career and apprentice opportunities, while building confidence and self esteem. A local cable television show created for teenagers was produced by the Education Helps' students. I have been a guest on the *Teen Talk* radio program, which is another means by which David reaches out to the youth in the community.

David is a hard working individual who would be an asset to any organization. I recommend him for employment without reservation. If you wish to discuss anything with me, please do not hesitate to contact me.

Sincerely,

John McKay

JM/pf

REPLY TO:
    ☐ Wildewood Professional Park, 3653 Cortez Road West, Suite 90, Bradenton, Florida 34210 (941) 727-6349
    ☐ 416 Senate Office Building, 404 South Monroe Street, Tallahassee, Florida 32399-1100 (850) 487-5078

Legislature's Website: *http://www.leg.state.fl.us*

TONI JENNINGS   WILLIAM G. "DOC" MYERS

18 Wall Street
Orlando, FL 32801

The Law Offices of Mark A. Fromang P.A.

(407) 540-1927
Fax (407) 540-1927

July 19, 2000

David Jonathan

    RE: State vs. Jonathan

Dear Mr. Jonathan,

    I have received your faxes requesting an update on your case. I called the Clerk of Court today to find out if there was any new court dates. I was told that there were no pending court appearances and that the State Attorney has not filed any information at this time.

    I will keep you updated as I receive information.

    Please feel free to call my office with any questions or concerns.

                Sincerely,

                MARK A. FROMANG

/krm

FLORIDA DEPARTMENT OF EDUCATION

JIM HORNE
Commissioner of Education

Just Read,
Florida!

July 15, 2004

Mr. David Jonathan
701 Willow Drive
Lehigh Acres, Florida 33936-6735

RE: Case Number: 034-2458-SA
SSN: ▮▮▮▮▮▮

Dear Mr. Jonathan:

Pursuant to the provisions of Sections 1012.56, 1012.796, and 1012.795, Florida Statutes, I have determined no probable cause to deny your application for a Florida Educator's Certificate. Accordingly, I am directing the Office of Professional Practices Services to prepare and make all required notices of this decision. My decision does not affect action by the Bureau of Educator Certification in determining your eligibility for certification or any action deemed appropriate by any local school district.

In finding no probable cause to deny your application, I do not intend to minimize the concerns raised by your law enforcement record. As Commissioner of Education, I am firmly committed to protecting the integrity of Florida's education profession. I urge you to uphold the highest ethical standards of the profession. Our children deserve nothing less. Be advised that a future violation of the professional standards can and will result in action against your certificate.

I wish you success in your teaching career. I encourage you to call on us for guidance and assistance in meeting the many challenges of your profession.

Sincerely,

Jim Horne

mwl/wj

FLORIDA DEPARTMENT OF
EDUCATION
fldoe.org

Pam Stewart
Commissioner of Education

~~June 23, 2014~~ Corrected Date: June 16, 2014

Ms. Shannon Smith
Interim Director of Personnel Services
2855 Colonial Boulevard
Fort Myers, Florida 33966

Re: David Jonathan
    Case No.: 134-3372
    DOE No.: 663863

Dear Ms. Smith:

The Office of Professional Practices Services received a report regarding the above referenced educator. Upon completion of the initial inquiry, this office has determined that further investigation is not warranted.

If this office can be of further assistance, please do not hesitate to contact us at 850-245-0438.

Sincerely,

Marian W. Lambeth

Fishing
Pond
at
the
Farmhouse

The Farmhouse
God gave to me
October 2000.
Located in
Pennsylvania.
PTL!

The house God gave to
me October 2000 in PA.

Pictured are Mother, Brother
and Sister-in Law.

August 8, 2005

Dear Mr. Jonathan:

Thank you so much for the clip highlighting my son and I at the Education Helps, Inc. TV shows. This was my son's first television interview, and we appreciate you sending it to us. All the best!

Sincerely,

JEB BUSH
GOVERNOR OF THE STATE OF FLORIDA

2011-12

FA911543W0   1086 K5J0223 E   79

Me, Looking like a Professor!

2008 Marjorie Crick Teacher of the year Award Nominee

FLORIDA COUNCIL FOR EXCEPTIONAL CHILDREN

In recognition of excellence in teaching students with disabilities

Presents this nominee award to

David Jonathan

Dr. Janet K. Lacey

FCEC President

OCTOBER 24, 2008

10/24/2008

Awards Chairman

OCTOBER 24, 2008

10/24/08

Council for Exceptional Children

The voice and vision of special education

Certificate of Recognition

Presented to

David Jonathan

Michigan International Academy

Nominated for 2007 Lee County Teacher of the Year

Presented by
The School Board of Lee County, Florida
This Thirteenth Day of March 2007

Jeanne S. Dozier
Chairman, District 2

Robert D. Chilmonik
District 1

Elinor C. Scricca, Ph.D.
District 5

Jane E. Kuckel, Ph.D.
Vice Chairman, District 3

Steven K. Teuber, J.D.
District 4

James W. Browder, Ed.D.
Superintendent

State of Florida

Department of Education

Temporary Educator's Certificate

This Certifies That

DAVID JONATHAN

*Has satisfactorily completed all requirements of law and State Board of
Education Rules for the coverages listed below:*

PHYSICAL EDUCATION (GRADES K - 12)
EXCEPTIONAL STUDENT EDUCATION (GRADES K - 12)

July 01, 2003–June 30, 2006

Department of Education Number 863803

Jim Warford
Chancellor, K-12 Public Schools

Jim Horne
Commissioner of Education

State of Florida Department of Education

PROFESSIONAL EDUCATOR'S CERTIFICATE

This Certifies That

DAVID JONATHAN

Has satisfactorily completed all requirements of Florida Statutes and State Board of Education Rules for the coverages or endorsements listed below:

ELEMENTARY EDUCATION / (GRADES K - 6)
EXCEPTIONAL STUDENT EDUCATION / (GRADES K - 12)

July 01, 2015 - June 30, 2020
Department of Education Number 663863

Brian Dassler
Deputy Chancellor for Educator Quality

Pam Stewart
Commissioner of Education

Issued June 05, 2014

CPSIA information can be obtained
at www.ICGtesting.com
Printed in the USA
FSOW02n0427130117
29431FS